demystifying purpose

10 pillars to eliminate emptiness and live a meaningful life

Simone Maria Quinn

demystifying purpose
Simone Maria Quinn

All rights reserved
First Edition, 2021
© Simone Maria Quinn, 2021
Cover image © Simone Maria Quinn

No part of this publication may be reproduced, or stored in a retrieval system, or transmitted in any form by means of electronic, mechanical, photocopying or otherwise, without prior written permission from the author.

The contents of this book have been certified and timestamped on the POA Network blockchain as a permanent proof of existence. Scan the QR code or visit the URL given on the back cover to verify the blockchain certification for this book.

The views expressed in this work are solely those of the author and do not reflect the views of the publisher, and the publisher hereby disclaims any responsibility for them.

Requests for permission should be addressed to
simonequinnauthor@gmail.com

ISBN - 978-0-6484884-9-1

Praise for Simone Maria Quinn and 'Demystifying Purpose'

Simone shares in this book a raw and heartfelt journey from feeling unfulfilled, frustrated and lost to falling back in love with herself and life, by changing the inner relationship with herself and how she saw herself and her life. She changed her reality and you can too.

If you, like Simone, have felt stuck trying to navigate through the rules, expectations and norms that society dictates, lost in the system of education, work, or parenthood that leaves you feeling inadequate and less, spending time and energy trying to satisfy other people's needs at the expense of yourself, then this book is for you.

Simone shows you through personal stories and practical tips how to navigate and embrace this thing called life, creating a life on your terms guided by meaning and purpose, and through the process of finding inner happiness and peace, and learning to enjoy the journey.

This is a great read and an encouraging book on how to discover your purpose and live a life of joy and happiness. A gift for everyone.

- Justine Robbins CEO Justine Robbins Consulting

'A thought provoking novella where the author's honest reflections encouraged me to reflect upon the decisions that I have made and that I do make in my life journey.'

- *Anonymous*

I found this book to be a clear roadmap to help navigate the reader through their own, unique life path. I liked the analogy of being in the 'driver's seat of our own lives' with the option to move forwards, backwards or to remain 'stuck' or motionless.

Concise guidelines offer the reader ways to overcome obstacles encountered on their journey with inspirational quotes from a variety of sources. The demystifying of purpose is explained and illustrated in ten chapters or 'pillars' with questions to help the reader look at their own particular roadblocks that are delaying them from connecting with the true essence of their lives and reaching their destination of purposeful, authentic living.

As a 'curious traveller' of your own life path, I found this book to be a clear, practical guide to help you overcome the obstacles that are preventing you from finding purpose in your life.

- Jo Hinchliffe, Living Purposefully at Lunasea

I dedicate this book to my loving family, who knew I had it in me.

Acknowledgments

A heartfelt thank you to my loving and supportive husband Dominique and my sister Damita for all your encouragement and support for which I am very grateful.

To my gifted book coach Shilpa Agarwal, who knew I had a story to share and encouraged me to write it and whose passion for storytelling is inspiring, thank you.

To the women who were in the writing group alongside me (Sujata, Sally-Ann, Sha, Shweta, and Swapna), it was a wonderful experience being on the journey with you all and to watch you and your books blossom.

With much gratitude to Jill, thank you for being there.

A big thank you to Jo Hinchliffe, Justine Robbins, and Julie Chambers for your friendships and for your support, insights, and wisdoms on my first book writing journey.

Foreword

Dear reader, what would it mean if you could get the advantage and wisdom of 30 years in 30 days or under?

What would it mean if you could get crisp cheat codes on discovering your life's purpose without having to spend 3 decades in a quest full of struggles?

If I've got your attention here, then it's for a very good reason. It is my honour to present to you Simone Maria Quinn's book 'Demystifying Purpose' which is a rich compilation of her lived experiences and which you can use as a guide to either find your purpose if you haven't landed on it yet or even to solidify and re-align with what truly matters to you if you've been dabbling with a few different ideas.

I first met Simone way back in 2017 via Facebook. Though we haven't had the chance to meet in person yet, over the last 6-7 months, we have met each other in the true sense - witnessing and sharing our tears, laughter, fears, desires and everything in between - while making this book a reality. As a book coach, nothing gives me more joy and contentment than to help birth one's untold stories on the pages of a book and to see the ripple effects that await the author. And to deliver this baby full of infinite potential, I'm a very proud book 'midwife'!

It is often said that 'one has a way with words' and though Simone has the gift of inspiring expression, it's refreshing how

DEMYSTIFYING PURPOSE

she NEVER minces her words, isn't afraid to speak her mind anymore (Read her book - and given where she started in her story, if she can arrive here, you can too.) and lives her life from a place of her truth rather than sugar-coating any facts or feedback for pleasing others. She doesn't explain where she doesn't need to and says just enough to move you into a state of bringing about change inspired from within. There was a reason I referred to this book earlier as 'crisp' cheat codes.

I would love to give you a taste of some golden nuggets from the book which I found very meaningful to apply in my life, and while I do that let me give you an overview of the journey that Simone has very carefully mapped out for her readers.
This book consists of 4 sections, i.e. Greatness, Gateway, Groundwork and Gifts.

Section 1 - Greatness - is all about the big picture - exploring the many options out there for you to choose from.
- 'Stuckness' is just a detour, but if you're willing to walk past the 5 'self' milestones Simone shares in **Chapter 1**, you're off to a great start!
- Have you ever felt that in your pursuit of belonging, you're now so lost in the crowd, that you have forgotten who you were without the social labels and without those with who you hang out? In **Chapter 2**, Simone, with her 6 ingredients helps you make the perfect recipe for 'YOU'niqueness so you can become fully aware again of who you are when you stand by yourself, and what is your unique contribution to the world.
- Her 'Enoughness' chapter (**Chapter 3**) is too close to my heart because it shares some of her childhood experiences and

DEMYSTIFYING PURPOSE

performance during school years - and it sounds like she's seen my childhood and read the mind of my teenaged self. I'm sure you will resonate with her pursuit of 'getting it right' because as humans, we all find ourselves walking that path of perfection at some point or the other in life. We all have countless defining moments in our life. What becomes a defining moment is something that is chosen unconsciously and we have very little control over, but what you do have now is the choice to decide what meaning you want to impart to those moments. And I'm confident you'll leave this chapter with a decluttered mind - at least I did when I read it!

- In life we often get get carried away in the pursuit of more, but **Chapter 4** 'Your WHY Matters' will help you get clear on your purpose statement and pursue that in life which truly matters to you and fulfilling your life's purpose.

Section 2 - Gateway - is an invitation to nail down what truly matters to you.

- **Chapters 5 and 6** about Identity and the Inner Compass are a natural extension of Chapter 4, wherein we start to get seriously up, close, and personal with what's within us rather than what's out there. That the secret to fully realising our life's purpose and potential lies within us is a life lesson I've learnt many times on repeat, and this reminder didn't hurt.

Section 3 - Groundwork - is all about taking responsibility and taking action by being in the driver's seat.
In **Chapters 7** & **8** Simone brings it down to simplistic actions that you can take here and now to awaken your potential.
In Chapter 7, the idea that stood out most for me was that courage

DEMYSTIFYING PURPOSE

doesn't have to be bold and loud, but can also appear in the form of baby steps grounded in hope. So if you're even slightly overwhelmed, read one paragraph, take one action, and progress will be made.

And what better to summarise Chapter 8 than Simone's equation on life: *Purpose + Potential = Meaningful Life = Story of One's Life*

Section 4 - Gifts - is all about embracing changes and as a result, enjoying the gift of your meaningful life.

The seeds of growth lie in facing challenges, overcoming resistance and embracing change so you can finally live your life on your purpose, and **Chapter 9** will show you how.

Chapter 10 then truly represents the vibe of 'giving' where Simone shows you how yo start living your truth and share your wisdom for others to benefit from.

And before I leave you, here is my favourite quote by Simone (from amongst many others you'll read in the book) which sums her up as well as her book, down to a T. It's simplicity inspires me to get out of any form of over-thinking or overwhelm and just get on with baby steps!

'You are unique plain and simple, so don't let your mind get in the way and mess things up.'

- Simone Maria Quinn

- Shilpa Agarwal
Book Coach
Chapter One Publishers

Introduction

'The purpose of life is to fully express oneself in one's unique way.'
- Simone Maria Quinn

Dear Reader,

Around the time I turned sixteen, I had to make some decisions about which subjects I would choose to study in grades 11 and 12 at secondary school. This is a big decision that teenagers face as they contemplate what they might do with their life as an adult, and their job and their career after joining the workforce. For me, this decision hinged on the question of what do I want to be when I grow up? At that young age, I had no idea.

I suffered great angst while choosing my subjects. I was good at sports, I liked English, History, and Biology, and I loved cooking, and that was about it. I had no idea what I wanted to be or do and I lacked self-confidence and had low self-esteem. After seeking some advice, I chose the subjects that were supposedly most likely to give me better opportunities in the future and help get a good job.

I chose mathematics and science with which I struggled because I found them hard and disinteresting. My self-belief took a nosedive in grade 11 and I began to believe that I was not good enough, which greatly affected my motivation to keep going. I completed grade 11, but could not go on to grade 12 at that time. So, I went looking for a job as my way out of school.

I signed up to become an indentured apprentice cook at an established restaurant located close to my high school. I was lucky enough to gain some work experience at the restaurant during the previous year. And thus began my 4-year cooking apprenticeship that commenced the week I turned eighteen, marking the beginning of my full-time career in the hospitality industry.

I completed my apprenticeship and, over the past 30 years, I have worked as a chef, but I have also taken time out to do other things. I completed my grade 12 through adult education and went on to complete an Economics Degree. I have worked in various roles in various sectors and went on to pursue further education, particularly in the area of personal development.

Approximately five years ago, I found myself reflecting on my life and how I was feeling emotionally and mentally. I was feeling frustrated, unfulfilled, disengaged, unmotivated, and stuck, and when I admitted it to myself, I realized I had been feeling like that for most of my life.

When I thought more about it, I was always feeling a dis-ease and anxiousness with my choices and decisions, and I began to realize that I had not yet found anything meaningful to me to do on my journey so far. My life path was fragmented and I'd been living with no real sense of direction - life had been doing me

DEMYSTIFYING PURPOSE

rather than me doing my life connected with my purpose.

I asked myself many questions like: Why do we do life and for what purpose? What does purpose mean? Is purpose and living a purposeful life significant? How does one find their purpose in life? What are the benefits of living a purposeful life?

I wrote this book because I wanted to share my learnings from my journey. It is never too late to connect with and live one's purpose and live a meaningful and fulfilling life.

I have found that we are born with our purpose and that some connect to their purpose early on in their life, while others connect with it later in life, and some never connect to their purpose for one reason or another.

In my book 'Demystifying Purpose', I mean to explore our unique traits (e.g. identity, standards, values, and beliefs) that exist within us and in which our purpose or reason for existing.

The book is divided into four sections: Greatness, Gateway, Groundwork, and Gifts, which comprise ten chapters (the ten pillars) that work together in communicating the message of the book, that is, by committing to the journey of getting to know and tapping into oneself, one will discover the purpose that they were born with. The job is to connect with one's purpose and pursue what is meaningful, and thus, live a fulfilling life rather than empty and meaningless.

If I knew in my younger years what I know now, I would have lived my life thus far with a lot less angst, gotten over myself a lot sooner, and wasted less time on endeavours that were not aligned with who I am. Also, I would have learned to start trusting my

DEMYSTIFYING PURPOSE

intuition and to trust myself, and to be truly living my purposeful life way earlier, resulting in being a happier version of myself.

Wherever you are on your path to connecting with your purpose, I hope that my insights are useful and of some value.

'For a long time, it had seemed to me that life was about to begin - real life. But there was always some obstacle in the way, something to be gotten through first, some unfinished business, time still to be served, or a debt to be paid. Then life would begin. At last, it dawned on me that this was my life. This perspective has helped me to see that there is no way to happiness. Happiness is the way. So treasure every moment you have and remember, time waits for no one.'

- Alfred Souza

CONTENTS

Part One   Greatness

1. Chapter 1: The Detour 2
2. Chapter 2: Embracing 'YOU'niqueness........................10
3. Chapter 3: Enoughness 20
4. Chapter 4: Your WHY Matters..32

Part Two   Gateway

5. Chapter 5: The Fabric of Identity....................................42
6. Chapter 6: Inner Compass..52

Part Three   Groundwork

7. Chapter 7: The Driver's Seat..62
8. Chapter 8: Awakening Potential......................................72

Part Four   Gifts

9. Chapter 9: Change - The Seed of Growth 84
10. Chapter 10: A Meaningful Life 94
11. My favourite quotes.. 102
12. References: 104

Part One

Greatness

Chapter 1: The Detour

'Life breaks us all and the best become strong in the broken places.'

– E. Hemingway

DEMYSTIFYING PURPOSE

This chapter explores the concept of how our path to our purpose may be broken, resulting in taking one detour after another, where one ends up in a place of not living their best life possible. Instead, one experiences unhappiness, shame, guilt, frustration, anxiety, resentfulness, unworthiness, and a feeling that they are not enough, and find themselves stuck because nothing changes.

What I mean by purpose is what we were born to be and do in the world before we got distracted and tuned out from ourselves and our true purpose path. I think it would be fair to speculate that a lot of people disconnect from themselves at some point in their lives. Some become unmotivated, disengaged, establish bad habits, and generally feel disempowered because they feel there are no other options or other choices available.

This feeling of being stuck can keep turning up, which makes sense, because the path one is on is broken when there has been a move further away from purpose. By moving away from purpose, one can find themselves going round in circles throughout their life bringing with it all kinds of struggles, hardships, and no movement forward in growth as a person, thus lacking fulfilment and meaning in their life.

' 'Stuckness' is simply a reluctance to take the next small step. Cut the next small step in half. Make the next step as small as you can. Then take it.'

- Martha Beck

I have, for most of my life, been living on the 'stuckness' carousel, which, at times, has left me feeling very unhappy, dis-empowered, ashamed, sad, and disengaged. I thought and believed there was something wrong with me, that I was not good enough, that I did not belong and fit in, and that life was just too damn hard.

I feel my path to my purpose was broken a long time ago, way back when I was a young child. There have been a few times in my life when I have wanted to give up but something within me always drove me to keep going, even though nothing made sense during those dark times.

Generally, everything seemed to become harder to do, like getting out of bed and attending to daily routine chores. I was never motivated and constantly feeling negative, my self-confidence hit rock bottom, I had very low self-esteem, felt unworthy, and found myself withdrawing from family and friends retreating into my little survival bubble.

About five years ago, I started on a journey to try to quell my confusion around the idea of 'myself'. I had been defining myself by what I did rather than who I was inside, what interested me, what I liked doing, and what fascinated me. I realized that did not know myself at all because I had unconsciously been focusing on pleasing and being liked. I had spent most of my life feeling like an imposter suffering from serious doses of lack of self-compassion, self-acceptance, self-love, self-belief, and self-trust.

I began to focus on these five areas of myself, which enabled me to slowly start moving through my state of stuckness and, step-by-step, create some momentum in moving forward to mending my path to my purpose.

I knew that if I did not start doing the work and taking the steps to heal and mend myself, the level of stuckness and the lack of worthiness would intensify and my life would just be on the repeat cycle and nothing would change.

Let's explore these five areas and how they can help with reconnecting with self, moving towards mending one's path to purpose, and to living a happier and meaningful life.

The five areas are:

1. Self-compassion

2. Self-love (self-care)

3. Self-acceptance

4. Self-belief

5. Self-trust

Self-compassion is where one extends compassion to one's self in instances where general suffering or feelings of inadequacy are perceived. Rather than being self-critical and ignoring our pain, we could be more understanding towards ourselves when we are suffering.

Being more compassionate to myself was a big step and hard for me as it made me feel more vulnerable and experience more pain. But feeling, being, and working through the pain helped with the mending process for me and I started liking myself.
I practice self-compassion by feeling and expressing gratitude, being more forgiving of myself, and being consistently mindful

DEMYSTIFYING PURPOSE

and present.

Self-love (self-care) means having regard for one's being and taking care of one's own needs and well-being with love towards self. In other words, not settling for less than what one deserves. The benefits of self-love are greater happiness, inner peace, increased motivation, stronger resilience, and better overall health.

I practice self-love by prioritizing 'me' time, like taking time out and doing things that bring me joy, and being honest with myself and others. I pay attention to my self-care routine, which involves good and regular sleeping patterns, having a relaxation ritual, healthy diet, and exercise, and replacing self-criticism with practicing gratitude. I also set boundaries around saying 'yes and no' for myself and when it comes to others, and when setting boundaries, I acknowledge how I am feeling at the time.

'If saying no to others means saying yes to yourself, you need to do it. Who will honour you if you yourself don't set an example for others on how you deserve to be treated?'

- Luminita D. Saviuc

Self-acceptance involves understanding oneself and being aware of one's strengths, weaknesses, capabilities, and embracing all facets of oneself that.

I find that self-acceptance is key for my mental health and wellness. I practice being kind to myself, learning to accept my imperfections, and staying positive, and I am more likely to confront my fears rather than give up without even trying.

DEMYSTIFYING PURPOSE

'Belonging starts with self-acceptance. Your level of belonging, in fact, can never be greater than your level of self-acceptance, because believing that you're enough is what gives you the courage to be authentic, vulnerable, and imperfect.'

– Brene Brown

Self-belief means believing in one's self, having confidence in one's abilities, and supporting themselves. Self-belief is vital because, without it, one may limit their opportunities, experiences and struggle to reach their full potential, and end up living an unfulfilling life.

I have been building on self-belief by caring for myself by paying attention to how I feel and acknowledging that. I have worked on not comparing myself to others, which has been a real eye-opener. I now set realistic and attainable goals, challenge myself without denigrating myself, and try to keep developing new skills, to gain new experiences, to keep on learning, and to just keep on working on myself. Learning to acknowledge my wins and losses and celebrate my accomplishments, no matter how small, has helped me too.

'Self-doubt is the most potent poison out there.'

- Kerwin Rae

Self-trust means trusting yourself and having a firm reliance on your integrity. I have learned to build self-trust by being kinder to myself, to keep my promises to myself, and to avoid compromising and undermining situations where possible.

DEMYSTIFYING PURPOSE

Self-trust, for me, means that I can overcome situations like failures and slip-ups, coping, following through, keep going and surviving. Self-trust and self-belief walk hand in hand.

With regards to myself, I have found that, by leaning in, going deep, and building on these five areas I have been able to slowly push through the 'stuckness' I've experienced in my life and become more confident and more aware as to what is going on internally and externally.

The benefits are that I am a happier and less anxious person. I feel more empowered to make better choices and decisions and more open to being curious and take risks. I am living with intention, I am more engaged and committed to myself, I feel worthy, and I am way more open to what is possible, which gives me hope.

When we are moving in the direction of mending our path and reconnecting with our selves we can start focusing on what does interest us and pay more attention to what fascinates us and spend more time on doing it.

Curiosity and courage are two important things I believe one needs to pursue and keep on doing what one finds meaningful and to face the fears and the obstacles that may arise while doing so.

I have found journaling a helpful way to release my thoughts, emotions, and confusion, and to connect with myself on a deeper level. By doing the internal work, I have witnessed my personal growth while connecting with myself and my purpose.

DEMYSTIFYING PURPOSE

Journal Prompts:

Below are journal prompts that I found useful and helpful in connecting with myself:

- What unique qualities do I have (and we all have them)?
- What am I curious about?
- What interests me?
- What is important to me?
- What do I value?
- What did I like doing as a child?
- My life is ideal when....?
- How do I best express myself?
- What hobbies do I have and which one would I choose if I had all the time in the world?
- What do I lose myself in?

'It's your place in the world; it's your life. Go on and do all you can with it, and make it the life you want to live.'

— Mae Jemison

Chapter 2: Embracing 'YOU'niqueness

'Since there is no one else like me in the entire universe…'The Magic' lies in my Uniqueness.'

- Simone Maria Quinn

DEMYSTIFYING PURPOSE

We are born unique in mind, body, and soul, and in this chapter, I explore the concept of uniqueness and its link to our purpose path.

We are all unique individuals with a unique purpose that we either acknowledge early in our lives or we spend a lifetime trying to find or, for some, never realize at all. Every single person is a unique canvas painted upon using various colours of DNA, personality, knowledge, talents, emotions, and feelings. Our perspectives, views, and behaviour are all unique and the journey of one's life is shaped by our interactions, experiences, choices, and decisions.

Being different is what we all are, but, ironically, there were times in my life when I wanted nothing more than to be like everyone else and presupposing that everyone was the same. Trying to be the same meant that I wanted the same experiences, results, outcomes, and achievements, but like our purpose, uniqueness does not condemn us to sameness.

By not embracing my uniqueness earlier in my life's journey, I inadvertently put my authentic self on the back burner as I tried to fit in and do the so-called right thing whatever I thought that was, and simply, just kept trying to get by. I would constantly compare myself with others which dis-empowered me in the process instead of me concentrating on my strengths, talents, and passions that were uniquely mine.

Comparing oneself with others is a futile and pointless exercise, because it is like comparing apples with oranges. But nothing about them is the same. The act of comparison leads to an illusion of one not being as good as another, which can have detrimental effects on how one experiences life. In my case, in some instances throughout my life, I just wouldn't even take the next step, or I would take a detrimental step because I believed I wasn't good enough, that I would not succeed, and then, I would find myself feeling discouraged and disappointed.

I now see my uniqueness as a strength and not something that does not belong or does not fit in the world. I know it takes courage to be who I am and not be too concerned about how I am received or even accepted. By embracing my uniqueness, I have become open to creating a life that puts me on the front burner of purpose and meaning and to keep on expanding and growing as I continue my life's journey, of which, happiness is a by-product.

Apart from our DNA and our physical body, many attributes make us different and our differences are valid, worth acknowledging, and embracing. Many aspects make us unique, and in the next part of this chapter, I will be exploring 6 such aspects that make us unique in the world. I liken these areas to being important metaphorical ingredients in the recipe of one's life. What we throw into the mix will determine the outcome, but can still be honed and improved depending on our desires, wants, needs and expectations.

The 6 aspects that make one unique:

1. Personality

2. Perspective

3. Attitude

DEMYSTIFYING PURPOSE

4. Experiences

5. Creativity

6. Passion

1. Personality

Our personality is uniquely our own. Personality is the characteristic pattern of thoughts, feelings, and behaviours that make a person unique. It is moulded from the moment we are born and remains fairly consistent throughout the journey of life.

No two people will have the exact same collection of knowledge, experiences, perceptions, and wisdom that allow us to be who we are. No two people are going to make the same choices or have the same response to experiences or share the same emotions and thoughts.

I began to truly embrace my personality over the last five years on my journey of self-acceptance and being enough. It was tiring trying to be someone who I was not, whilst at the same time, the authentic me was screaming out for acknowledgment by me. I found trying to be anything but me confusing, frustrating, and damaging where ultimately I was being disrespectful towards myself.

I realized that people will either be drawn to me or not because of my personality and that is okay, as it is not a reflection of who I am. Now, from a place of self-love and respect, I proudly take on board all the facets of my personality because, quite simply, I am who I am!

2. Perspective

The way one sees the world (their perception) and the way one sees one's self is unique. The way we live, what we experience and the knowledge we have is not the same as anyone else. My perception is uniquely my own and can be developed by having an open mind, listening, and reading, and by acknowledging other people's opinions, ideas, and wisdom.
I remind myself that my perspective is about how I perceive something to be or how I choose to see something, which then becomes my truth and my story. But, it doesn't mean that it is true for anyone else.

When I can't change a situation in my life, I change my perspective, like altering a lens on a camera and reframing how I am viewing the situation. I have found that the more open-minded I am and the less judgemental I become, the more positive my perspective is concerning my experiences and I am able to move on more quickly.

3. Attitude

One's attitude is something that is influenced and formed by their emotional environments and is dictated by how one perceives life and by the actions of others.
I know that I can choose to have a positive or a negative attitude and that either one will affect and influence other people around me. In recent years, I have questioned myself when I have been feeling negative with regards to experiences or other people and noticed how occupied I'd become with my thoughts.
I know now that I can make an active choice to change my

attitude to one that is more conducive to being positive and happier and that will alter the quality of my experiences and enhance what I want to accomplish in my life.

4. Experiences

Experiences (both good and challenging) can influence, shape, and help one grow as a person. How one experiences the experience is unique, which affects how one interacts with other people and how they navigate their way through life. Our experiences can be both negative and positive and how we choose to respond to them is unique to us too.

I appreciate that I've acquired a lot of wisdom from my experiences where, for some, I am very grateful, while others, I could have done without.

Nevertheless, what has happened in the past has been and gone. Now, I am well-equipped to ask better questions of myself and others and make better decisions in pursuing a more meaningful life.

5. Creativity

There are so many forms of creativity, e.g. writing, painting, drawing, singing, designing, building, arranging, etc. Everyone has their own unique and creative gifts that are influenced by their inner vision and perception of what is pleasing to them, what they find beautiful, and what they like doing naturally or with ease. Creativity is a real form of self-expression that encompasses a style that is uniquely one's own.

Over my growth period from child to adult, I held a belief that, to be creative, one had to be good at something before pursuing that outlet. I believed I was not creative and not very good at anything except cooking and experimenting with different ingredients as it turns out. Only recently have I acknowledged that I am creative in the kitchen and when not under pressure from time constraints that I enjoy the creative process.

Over the last ten years or so, I started to develop an interest in gardening, but I was not confident to start making decisions in that area because I believed I was not good enough and I wouldn't get it right. Fast forward to current times, with my updated self-beliefs, I am witnessing my garden flourishing and coming into its own, because I let go of my self-imposed restrictions and creatively kept planting by trial and error that gave me joy.

I realized it is the starting and the doing that things evolve through the creative process and that exploring my creative side is like being a kid again when I would just let go, because, in the end, it is for my betterment.

'What strikes me is the fact that, in our society, art has become something which is related only to objects and not to individuals, or to life. That art is something that is specialised or which is done by experts who are artists. But couldn't everyone's life become a work of art? Why should the lamp or the house be an object of art, but not our life?'

– Michael Foucault

6. Passion

Passion is a big part of the human experience that drives one toward what they want to do and achieve. Our passions can stir

DEMYSTIFYING PURPOSE

our emotions that can enable us to step outside of our comfort zone and do that thing we thought we could never or would ever do Passion can drive one to set goals and tasks, keep to routines and determine one's quality of life, and can illuminate our path in life where we can truly contribute to the world in our unique way.

I have come to believe that self-belief plays a big part in pursuing one's passion, as has been my experience. Instead of worrying about what other people might think or whether or not things worked out or not, I started letting go of the illusion of perfection and began with little steps with projects I had a passion for and that gave me joy.

By acknowledging and harnessing our uniqueness and accepting the uniqueness of others, just imagine what is possible and the impactful experiences that one would have during one's journey of their life.

'You are unique plain and simple, so don't let your mind get in the way and mess things up.'

- Simone Maria Quinn

DEMYSTIFYING PURPOSE

Journal Prompts:

Below are some journal prompts I found useful with regards to tapping into my uniqueness.
Hopefully, you will also find these prompts a useful exercise in witnessing your uniqueness as I have.

- What do you like to do?

- Notice... what do you like/love?

- What are you passionate about?

- What makes you feel authentic?

- What does your ideal day look like?

- What do you like about yourself?

- Ask others close to you...what they like/love about you?

- What makes your heart sing?

- Where is your happy place?

- Who do you love spending time with?

'You are unique and if that is not fulfilled then something has been lost.'

- Martha Graham

Chapter 3: Enoughness

'Many of us will spend our entire lives trying to slog through the shame swampland to get to a place where we can give ourselves permission to be both imperfect and to believe we are enough.'

- Brene Brown

DEMYSTIFYING PURPOSE

The concept of 'Enoughness' is the sense of one's perception of being enough or being good enough. The fear of not being good enough or not being enough is one of the universal fears that plagues most people at some stage in their life or most of their life.

Not being good enough is a belief that we have about ourselves either from external or internal influences or both. Simply, what we assume or what we tell ourselves we start to believe is true. One continues to find evidence to back up the belief of which becomes one's reality until one tells oneself otherwise.

Imagine what would happen if one tore up an existing belief they have of themselves, e.g. 'I am not good enough', and created a new belief, e.g. 'I am enough and I am grateful for that', and truly believed and embraced it. Imagine how one would feel and see themselves in their future world, the new energy that they would exude, and their changed perception of their reality.

For a very long time, I held a belief that I was not very smart and that I was not a good learner compared to other people. I remember, when I was at primary school, sometimes we'd have to answer general knowledge questions out loud in front of the class. One time when I got few answers wrong, I was laughed at, and I felt stupid and became very anxious at the thought of having to answer any more questions. For most of my life, I was riddled with fear of being put on the spot to answer questions because I didn't want to get it wrong.

The learning journey throughout my school years was not an easy one because I believed I was not good enough. I self-sabotaged by procrastinating and left completing school work till the last minute, because I feared not getting it right, which made me feel anxious.

When in high school, I chose the subjects that I would never excel in and, in some cases, failed, because I felt the pressure to do what seemed right instead of listening to my intuition and trusting myself. In doing so, I reinforced my belief that I was not good enough. Now, I see that, by not listening to my intuition, I did not trust myself, and I did not trust myself because I believed I was not good enough.

I have doubted myself and my abilities for the majority of my life and, in doing so, have made poor choices at times and put off making decisions that seemed too hard to make. From around the age of 15 up until about 5 years ago, I have been rendered stuck in a vicious cycle of self-doubt, low self-esteem, indecision, procrastination, dis-empowerment, and a general lack of self-appreciation. So, for me, something had to change internally concerning my thoughts and beliefs about myself for me to start making empowered and quality choices that reinforced my new belief that I am enough (always was and always will be), no matter what.

'You are enough...If you were to be any more than you are then you would be... honour yourself.'

- Simone Maria Quinn

What does being enough mean?

Being enough, for me, means embracing and owning

DEMYSTIFYING PURPOSE

everything about me and being proud of who I am, no matter what anyone else may say or think, and that I belong.

Someone else's opinion and what they say about you is none of your business. What is important is the attention one pays towards self with regards to kind self-talk and being mindful of the negative thoughts and beliefs that may arise for whatever reason.

Being enough means that one is happy and grateful for who they are and that they embrace all that they are, e.g. their abilities, inabilities, successes, failures, passions, gifts, interests, likes, dislikes, what they look like, where they've come from, etc.

Being enough does not mean that there is nothing more to learn, nothing further to achieve or improve on, nowhere to grow to, and that one can't ask for help. Being enough means that one accepts, values, respects and believes in self as one navigates one's life given all the distractions, detours, and deviations along the way.

'Whatever you hold in your mind consistently is exactly what you will experience in your life.'

- Tony Robbins

Why does one not feel enough?

There are various reasons why one grapples with the limiting belief or fear of not being enough or being good enough. The seed can be sown from a very young age and compounded further as the years go on or until one changes their belief.

DEMYSTIFYING PURPOSE

We can experience particular events in our lives way back in our youth when we've had difficulty sorting through the thoughts, feelings, and emotions that arise. Consequently, we tell ourselves stories about what that experience meant and find it impossible to separate ourselves from the experience, thus not being able to move forward. One can be crippled with self-doubt, low self-esteem, leaving one disillusioned, frustrated, sad, and vulnerable.

There is no getting it right or getting it wrong with being enough or feeling enough. It simply comes down to one's belief about self and not what one perceives themselves.

I know that being enough and good enough is an inside job and to not let externalities dictate otherwise, because we are all enough and we matter.

'I'm a big believer in accepting yourself and not really worrying about it.'

- Jennifer Lawrence

In the next part of this chapter, I will explore 4 areas that can feed one's belief of not being enough.

The four areas are:

1. Perfectionism

2. Comparisons

3. People Pleasing

DEMYSTIFYING PURPOSE

4. Imposter Syndrome

1. Perfectionism

Perfectionism is to appear perfect or the act of achieving perfection where one desires to be the best by setting up unrealistic high standards of oneself (and in some cases others) that can never be achieved.

There are no allowances for mistakes when striving for perfection. So, when mistakes are made, they can be seen as flaws rather than something that can be learned from. The illusion of perfection can set one up to be self-critical, never feeling or being good enough, anxious, and feeling a false sense of being in control.

I have run a perfectionist strategy in certain areas of my life for most of my life, and I have suffered the effects from it, like procrastination and inaction, which leads to not starting and not finishing well, anxiety, and unwarranted stress.

I now see that choosing to be human with all my imperfections over being perfect, appreciating, embracing, and being grateful for all that I am has contributed to my healthier sense of self-worth, thereby opening the door to more joy and meaning in my life.

'To be yourself in a world that is constantly trying to make you something else is the greatest accomplishment.'

- Ralph Waldo Emerson

DEMYSTIFYING PURPOSE

2. Comparisons

Comparing one's self to others is like comparing the sun with the moon… there is no comparison. So, what is the point?

I believe we're all born with our unique gifts, all with an individual purposes to offer the world and to make a contribution. In my experience, when we start comparing ourselves with others, we diminish or cancel ourselves out by giving away our power, our strengths, and our uniqueness, which can lead to low self-esteem and reinforce the belief of not being good enough and that one does not belong.

I accept that the only person I would ever compare myself to is the person I was yesterday, while reminding myself that I can only do my best with what I have and to be grateful for that.

'Comparison is the death of joy, and the only person you need to be better than is the one you were yesterday.'

- Rachel Hollis

3. People Pleasing

People-pleasing (also known as co-dependency or anxious attachment) is about fitting in and putting others' wants, needs, and happiness before one's own as a result of not feeling good enough to consider themselves before others.

Low self-esteem, feeling insecure, looking for acceptance, need for control, and overachieving are generally the key ingredients for one who is a people-pleaser and this is generally accompanied by perfectionism, anxiety, sadness, and anger.

DEMYSTIFYING PURPOSE

I can relate to people-pleasing. I have been a people pleaser since I was a child, which had not served me well before I decided to start respecting myself. When I acknowledged that I was a people pleaser that was the first step to making changes in my life. I needed to make changes in what I believed about myself and to start accepting and respecting myself which was not easy and it did not happen overnight. If I had not made inroads to changing I would still be sad, angry, and despondent.

If one can take the first small step in making sustainable changes in the self-belief department (like I have) and move away from trying to please others first, they will slowly feel empowered, build up their self-esteem and confidence and no longer feel the need to keep looking for approval from others to feel that are enough.

'Caution:
If you trade in your authenticity for being liked, you may experience the following:
Anxiety, depression, addiction, rage, blame, resentment, and inexplicable grief.'

- Brene Brown

4. Imposter Syndrome

The definition of imposter syndrome according to the Oxford Dictionary:

Noun: ***imposter syndrome***
- The persistent inability to believe that one's success is deserved or has been legitimately achieved as a result of one's own efforts or skills.

DEMYSTIFYING PURPOSE

- People suffering from impostor syndrome may be at an increased risk of anxiety.

Imposter syndrome is where one internalizes the feeling of being a fraud and being found out, constantly doubting one's talents, gifts, and accomplishments, thus reinforcing the belief of not being good enough and is generally exacerbated by perfectionism.

When it comes to combating imposter syndrome, one needs to start believing in themselves and rewire their brain to eliminate anxiety-producing thoughts and replace them with confidence-boosting thoughts.

I have indeed been plagued with imposter syndrome throughout my life where it has rendered me frozen of choice, leaving me feeling helpless, not good enough, and wanting to hide from the world.

I have done a lot of work on myself with regards to acknowledging and eliminating the anxious thoughts that would come up for me and change the way I think, to thinking more positively. I found that doing this exercise as quickly as possible is key to moving through and out the other side of the feeling of an imposter. I have learned that there is always another way of looking at something, which is key to ultimately changing my perspective, believing I'm good enough, feeling comfortable in my skin, and knowing there is nothing wrong with me. I have concluded that self-acceptance is the antidote to imposter syndrome.

DEMYSTIFYING PURPOSE

'Unlike guilt, which is the feeling of doing something wrong, shame is the feeling of being something wrong.'

- Marilyn J. Sorensen

First and foremost, one must matter to one's self and know that they matter. One must pay attention to the messages they tell themselves and re-frame where necessary, replacing limiting beliefs with new beliefs with positive intent and taking comfort in the fact that we are enough.

Following are examples of some limiting beliefs that I have held about myself in the past that I believed was true. Over time, I have learned to reframe or rephrase the limiting belief that would come up for me, work to replace it with a positive belief, and then, start building the muscle around that new belief.

On one hand, it is not so easy to change a belief. But, on the other hand, a belief is just a belief and I am now more mindful as to how much thought is given to a negative belief I may have about myself.

DEMYSTIFYING PURPOSE

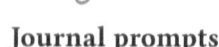

Journal prompts:

As an exercise, ponder over the examples below of some negative beliefs and write down what would be a more positive and empowering belief instead.

I have found that writing down negative beliefs first and tearing them up and throwing those away before writing down new positive beliefs is very helpful in moving forward to being enough.

- I'm not good with money…
- I'm not attractive…
- I can't do it because…
- I am not smart…
- I never get anything right…
- I will never be successful…
- I am not deserving…
- My life will never get any better…
- I am not lovable because…
- I am ashamed of myself…
- I'm not qualified…
- I am not experienced…

DEMYSTIFYING PURPOSE

- People will judge me...

- I could've done better...

- I should've known better...

'The energy it takes to hang onto the past is holding you back from a new life.'

- Mary Manin Morrissey

Chapter 4: Your WHY Matters

'It's not what you do, it's why you do it that makes the difference'

- Brene Brown

DEMYSTIFYING PURPOSE

This chapter explores the importance of knowing our why... our purpose... and how it helps with pursuing a meaningful life, living with integrity, and experiencing fulfilment.

Our why is a part of who we are and what we stand for and it matters because it drives one's focus, thoughts, and actions. It helps one truly express who they are, get to know themselves, and make it easier to live a life aligned with their core values.

One might know what they are doing and how they are doing it but not be so clear on why they are doing it. The why is the inspirational part of the doing - the vision that will keep one going, given all the obstacles and difficulties that may be faced.

If one doesn't know their why or have any purpose, it is perhaps because they don't know or have not worked out what is important to them and what they truly value. By not knowing what one values, they can essentially, and without realizing it, take on other people's values that are not in alignment with who they are.

Other people's priorities, needs, and wants can inadvertently become our own, which ultimately influences the choices and decisions one makes. As a result, one can become increasingly lost, confused, and unfocused; have negative thoughts; disengage; and have no drive or reason to move forward and live life purposefully.

For most of my life, I had not been in touch with my values, and so, I mostly felt lost, confused, unmotivated, stuck, and not living life with any particular focus or intention. When I look back, I realize that I had been living life in survival mode, staying busy in the doing without an ounce of self-awareness. I was constantly searching for validation, looking externally for answers, and making unresourceful choices and decisions leading to frustration, disempowerment, and sadness. For one reason or another I could not or would not go within to find what it was I was here to do and to honour and trust myself in the process of connecting with my purpose.

When something is broken, it may only barely work or not work at all. It needs mending and the pieces put back together so it can operate at optimum levels. I tried putting myself back together multiple times over the years but the strategies I employed only worked on the surface. Deep down inside was where the work needed to be done, and that was the difficult bit.

Even though I felt broken I now know that I wasn't broken but that I hadn't been living aligned with who I am and what I value. Doing the work was hard and painful as it required me to have courage, be vulnerable in my quest to make the internal shift, and upgrade to my authentically aligned operating platform.

The next part of this chapter explores key factors:

1. Discovering your why.

2. Why pursue what is 'Meaningful' to you?

3. Creating a 'Why' or 'Purpose' Statement.

'To love what you do and feel that it matters...how could anything be more fun.'

- Katherine Graham

DEMYSTIFYING PURPOSE

1. Discovering your Why

Discovering one's why may not be so easy and it can take time involving some degree of work and action to peel away the proverbial layers until there is clarity around the why...the purpose of the life one has been given. Our why is not just about us, it is bigger than us and bigger than others around us. It connects us to what we care about, it is about how we spend our time, how we contribute, and what kind of impact it will have in the overall bigger picture of our life.

Below are some questions I began asking myself that assisted me with getting closer to my purpose in making my life a better one.
Perhaps take a moment and read the questions, observe your answers concerning yourself and notice what comes up for you.

Questions:

- What lights you up and makes you feel alive?
- What are you curious about?
- What inspires you?
- What are you passionate about?
- What is meaningful to you?
- What do you value?
- What do you feel connected to?
- What do you care about?

DEMYSTIFYING PURPOSE

- What matters to you?
- What are your strengths?
- What are you good at?
- Where do you add value?
- How will you measure your life?
- What do you want to leave (your contribution) as your legacy?

'Simply, if one could meet the needs of the world by pursuing their strengths, then one would be living their why.'

- Simone Maria Quinn

2. Why pursue what is 'meaningful' to you?

One can be inspired by something where there is an inner feeling or a wanting to act and do something. One must also be motivated, to have a reason to act to push past any obstacles or challenges that may present while moving forward and pursuing something meaningful. I have found that there can be no greater reward than to pursue what one finds meaningful. It reflects the how and why one spends their time. It also expands their comfort zone, which leads to personal growth.

When we pursue what is meaningful to us, there is clarity in thinking, decision making, and choices and in taking action. One is better prepared to learn from their mistakes, deal with letdowns, rejections, and setbacks, let go, move on, bounce back and try again.

When we know our why and pursue what is meaningful, we can make plans, set goals and benchmarks, be productive, contribute, have fun and enjoy and be open to life. The ripple effects of pursuing what we find meaningful are endless, rewarding, and could make a difference and add value to other people's lives.

'Concentrate all of your efforts on one definite chief aim.'

- Napoleon Hill

3. Creating a 'Why' or a 'Purpose' Statement

Writing one's own 'Why' or 'Purpose' statement can help achieve clarity around their why and know what they want to do and who they genuinely and authentically need to be. A 'Why' statement helps with staying focused and keeping one's attention on the tasks and activities that will connect to that of which one cares about. Having a 'Why' statement can be the game-changer that determines the meaning and quality of one's life and I believe it is a good idea to review and update the statement from time to time as one grows and evolves.

When one is clear on their why, it is a matter of the 'how' and 'what else' that might be of benefit in one's pursuit on what matters to them most moving forward and stepping into who they are because they know 'why'.

DEMYSTIFYING PURPOSE

Our 'Why or Purpose' statement clearly states an actionable contribution that one wants to make an impact or a difference in the world using language that resonates with the one writing the statement.

The statement can be revisited, refined, and updated as one grows and evolves on their journey of life.

DEMYSTIFYING PURPOSE

As an exercise, try writing your 'Why Statement' concerning your life and see what you come up with and observe where you are now and what could be the first step in embodying and living your 'why'.

'Find your why and you will find your way.'

- John C. Maxwell

Part Two

Gateway

Chapter 5: The Fabric of Identity

'It is not until you change your identity to match your life blueprint that you will understand why everything in the past never worked.'

- Shannon L. Alder

DEMYSTIFYING PURPOSE

One's identity is composed of three parts; personal identity, family identity, and social identity. In this chapter, I will be focusing on personal identity, and within that, self-identity. There are many elements that make up our personal identity, i.e., who one is as an individual. Some of these elements include standards, beliefs, needs, values, virtues, attitudes, principles, dreams, personality, habits, experiences, goals, interests, wants, talents, abilities, career, job, physical features, thoughts, feelings, emotions, behaviour, and actions.

Self-identity is one's perception of self and connection with self. Self-identity is the image one has of themselves, which affects how they might feel and behave in any given situation and experience throughout their life. It is not uncommon that one identifies one's self only as being some parts of their personal identity, e.g. their physical features or their career that can, in their mind, define who they think they are. This can be very confusing and one who is only focusing on the external parts of themselves and not considering inner elements of themselves could suffer from an identity crisis.

In my experience, having a healthy perspective on my personal identity where I consistently check in with myself to refine, upgrade, and get rid of what no longer serves benefits my perception of my self-image. When I have a healthy and realistic image of myself, I am more likely to be living aligned with who I truly am and be more likely to connect to my purpose with more ease.

When I think about my earlier life I never really thought about setting standards for myself, checking in on my thoughts, beliefs, values, habits, and actions. I was more or less occupied with meeting my basic needs and trying to get through the days, the weeks, and the years as best as I could. My self-identity was caught up in my work and the busier I was the more evidence I had with regard to who I thought I was and only identified with that person. But, I was not connecting with all of the elements of who I was, nor was I meeting all my needs. So, I eventually found myself spirally downward into a heap of exhaustion, an emotional mess, and experiencing burnout a few times over.

It got to a point where I was so confused about who I was and what I was here to do that I was forced to stop and literally take stock and do some really uncomfortable personal work, which I now call self-investment. Over a period of time, I realized that my work and my job did not define who I was, where I had been interpreting the doing part as the being part of me. I now know that there many aspects of me that are me, like my beliefs, values, needs, wants, hobbies, abilities, interests, experiences, feelings, and emotions, and I have learned to embrace them as a part of my identity too.

'Identity cannot be found or fabricated but emerges from within when one has the courage to let go.'

- Doug Cooper

In the next part of this chapter, I will explore the personal identity part by looking at three filters by which one uniquely sees the world and that affect how one behaves in the world.

DEMYSTIFYING PURPOSE

The three filters are:

1. Personal Standards

2. Beliefs

3. Needs

1. Personal Standards

'If you don't set a baseline standard for what you'll accept in life, you'll find it easy to slip into behaviours and attitudes or a quality of life that's far below what you deserve.'

- Tony Robbins

Personal standards are a set of behaviours based on values, beliefs, needs, and wants that one chooses to consistently give way to and they are built upon one's expectations of oneself. The behaviours determine one's actions and results, such as settings boundaries, reaching certain goals, the quality of life, and level of self-fulfilment. Standards are benchmarks for how one treats self and others and how one consistently reflects one's integrity, self-esteem, and self-respect.

One can set negotiable and non-negotiable standards when it comes to self by getting clarity on what they want to achieve, how to make that a reality, and how to stay self-accountable. The questions to ask are: If one did not set personal standards what would their life look like, how would one feel about one's self and what choices would they be making.

As I have found, personal standards can be set for any area of one's life. Consciously setting good standards and sticking to them is important because they help in making good decisions and better choices that align with who one is. Standards can always be evaluated and raised for achieving one's goals, making changes, and living a more fulfilling and happy life.

I Choose...
To live by choice, not by chance;
To make changes, not excuses;
To be motivated, not manipulated;
To be useful, not used;
To excel, not compete.
I choose self-esteem, not self-pity.
I choose to listen to my inner voice,
Not the random opinion of others.

- The Stencilsmith

2. Beliefs

'If you accept a limiting belief, then it will become a truth for you.'

- Louise Hay

Beliefs are what one feels or holds to be true about oneself and about how the world works even without proof. One's beliefs are generally formulated in the early stages of life from experiences, incidents, upbringing, faith, and religion, etc.

There are social beliefs as in what one believes about others, i.e., the social norm, and there are personal beliefs with regards to self-belief and attitude towards oneself. Our thoughts become

DEMYSTIFYING PURPOSE

our beliefs that become the words, both positive and negative, we tell ourselves that determine our actions, inactions, habits, choices and what we care about.

'Your beliefs become your thoughts.
Your thoughts become your words.
Your words become your actions.
Your actions become your habits.
Your habits become your values.
Your values become your destiny'

– Mahatma Gandhi

One can have self-limiting beliefs that hold them back where these beliefs are fed with negative thinking and negative self-talk, resulting in low self-esteem and keeping one from achieving and experiencing a fulfilling life.

Examples of self-limiting beliefs are: I am not good enough, I am not worthy, I am useless and I am unlovable.

As with any beliefs, limiting self-beliefs can be changed and replaced with new empowering self-beliefs, but, for that to happen, requires personal inner work and determination to make the change.

I have found that change requires establishing and building self-trust, self-confidence, and self-worth. It also requires keeping promises to one's self and creating new habits in establishing a life in which one feels self-empowered, where one has a choice, and ultimately, the fortitude to decide on how much one values oneself.

DEMYSTIFYING PURPOSE

My self-belief journey has had its uneasy moments and there have been many times when the 'too hard' beliefs would kick in, and then, I would ask myself why bother and who cares? But I worked out that, if I did not care about myself or believe in myself, then I was limiting myself from experiencing a better life - a life that was not just about myself but also about others.

'Once we believe in ourselves, we can risk curiosity, wonder, spontaneous delight, or any experience that reveals the human spirit.'

- E.E. Cummings

3. Needs

'Your life purpose is a blend of your core personality needs. Remember it, define it and refine it as you journey through life.'

- Diana Dentinger

Needs are things that are necessary in order for one to live a healthy life and any deficiencies in needs being met can ultimately cause adverse and severe outcomes. Everybody has psychological (spiritual) and material needs to be attended to and prioritized with regard to the direction of their life.

In 1943, American psychologist Abraham Maslow created the Hierarchy (or Pyramid) of Needs known universally as 'Maslow's Hierarchy of Needs'. This concept of needs emerged when Maslow was looking for the meaning of life and what could make life purposeful for people.

The theory behind the pyramid is that people are motivated by five categories of needs ranging from basic needs through to higher psychological and spiritual needs. One's basic needs, such as physiological and safety needs, must be looked after first before being able to pay attention to one's psychological needs, such as belonging, being loved and esteem needs, and then, finally moving towards self-fulfilment needs and where one has a sense of self-identity.

'Maslow's Hierarchy of Needs'

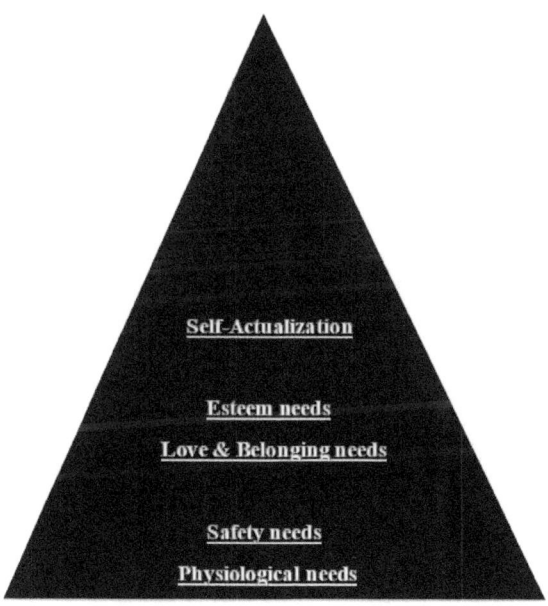

The pyramid illustrates how life can be lived in harmony given the complexities of human nature, where one can use the tool to focus on what to do next in trying to balance all of one's needs. Once one's physiological needs, safety needs, and psychological needs are met, one can move towards achieving one's full potential and knowing thy self.

Most importantly, one gets to realize that life is about others as well, and thus, contributing and adding value to others becomes an integral and natural part of one's life, which results in personal development, where one is continually growing and evolving in one's quest for a meaningful life.

'The good or healthy society would then be defined as one that permitted people's highest purposes to emerge by satisfying all their basic needs.'

- Abraham Maslow

DEMYSTIFYING PURPOSE

Exercise:

Personal Standards:

Standards start with self before others.

As an exercise, think about and write down what is negotiable and what is non-negotiable when it comes to your own standards for yourself and with regards to others when making choices and decisions in your life.

Beliefs:

Beliefs are what we feel certain about.

Write down your top 10 beliefs that you believe are true about yourself.
They can be both limiting and positive beliefs.
Observe what comes up for you particularly around any negative beliefs.
Try replacing any negative beliefs with positive beliefs with the aim of those positive beliefs becoming your actual beliefs about yourself.

Chapter 6: Inner Compass

'To Know Thy Self is the beginning of Wisdom.'

- Socrates

DEMYSTIFYING PURPOSE

The inner compass is about one's true essence where trusting our intuition and living in alignment with our values and virtues is paramount to living our authentic, fulfilled, and emotionally well life.

We can look at life as a journey but it is how one travels internally that will ultimately determine the quality of their experiences and how they feel about it. Life can throw all kinds of obstacles and adversities that can shake one's life around a bit or a lot and the key to responding is how truly one is connected with one's self.

Being connected means gathering and using knowledge, being self-aware, and getting clarity with regards to what one values and what matters. If one lives according to another's values and expectations, through lack of self-belief, self-doubt and self-trust, then one can easily succumb to getting off track and get distracted from their life's purpose resulting in life getting a little messy at times.

Looking externally to fulfil my needs, wants, and desires was my modus operandi throughout most of my life, which I can honestly say that, overall, did not serve me well. Eventually, it got to a point where I found myself running on empty spiritually and emotionally and I was questioning my existence and the meaning and the point of my life.

I was completely disconnected within, confused and lost and I knew I had to do something to change how I perceived myself and what about that seemed unbearable to live with daily. I had to dare to dig in deep and reconnect with my inner self and resolve the mystery of my existence to establish self-trust and improve self-belief.

This internal rectification was a long and, at times, painful journey as I had to go places within me that I had never been to - where I had to feel, resolve and heal. Today, I stand clearer on what matters to me, what I value and how I live by those values, trusting myself, living emotionally well, and happily knowing why I am here.

The next part of this chapter explores what constitutes the core of who we are by way of three key internal filters that guide one like an actual compass that points in the right direction if they so choose to take it.

The three filters are:

1. Inner guide (intuition)

2. Values

3. Virtues

1. Inner guide

I refer to the inner guide as being one's intuition where intuition is ones perception or insight of truth without needing evidence or data and that it is also independent of any reasoning. Intuition is also known as gut feeling where one is aware of a situation intuitively.

Intuition is all about stability and abundance, where one is feeling confident in making a choice or a decision about something and that they are inspired and excited if it involves something good. Trusting and being guided by one's intuition is a lot easier said than done because ego is always there to test and feed the inner critic.

Ego is driven by fear and a scarcity mindset and the inner critic or voice starts to question ideas, indecisive about viewpoints, and uses inconsistent language displaying a lack of self-trust. Ego is very dominant and controlling as its main job is to protect us and keep us safe from anything new or different.

The interesting thing about intuition and ego is that they always present and one's challenge is to quieten the ego down long enough to let intuition guide one back to one's highest purpose.

It would be fair to say that I've mainly been guided by my ego over the years simply because I haven't trusted myself enough and was more concerned about doing the right thing. I know now that my intuition is more of a safe bet when making choices and decisions, as it disallows the head chatter and the overthinking.

'The more you trust your intuition, the more empowered you become, the stronger you become, and the happier you become.'

- Gisele Bundchen

2. Values

One is born with values and those values live in our heart, not in our head, and are there to be discovered as one grows and evolves. Values are what matter to us, they are our emotional and moral compass that guide and influence how we live our life.

DEMYSTIFYING PURPOSE

To be aligned with one's values means that one feels great, emotionally well, and is in a good place to make mindful decisions and choices and to live a fulfilled and happy life. Life can be challenging at times, but, as one grows into one's self, develops a healthy perspective, and has integrity towards self, they become clearer on what matters.

'Integrity
Choosing courage over comfort;
Choosing what is right over what is fun, fast or easy;
And choosing to practice our values rather than simply professing them.'

– Brene Brown

I think that the ultimate test to gauge whether one is living in alignment with one's values is how one is feeling. If one is feeling crappy in one or more areas of their life most of the time, then it may be a sign that one is not living in alignment with their values.

One can unveil and connect with their values by observing their strengths, talents, abilities, behaviour, personality, standards, virtues, motivations, interests, and passions.

Some examples of my values are:

- Family
- Love
- Connection
- Health and vitality

DEMYSTIFYING PURPOSE

- Compassion
- Trust
- Happiness
- Freedom
- Security

'The more you choose moves that are towards your values, the more vital, effective and meaningful your life is likely to become.'

- Susan David

3. Virtues

'Love is the virtue of the heart, sincerity is the virtue of the mind, decision is the virtue of the will, and courage is the virtue of the spirit.'

- Frank Lloyd Wright

Virtues are ideals or standards that one works towards with good moral qualities and it is our values that guide us towards achieving those standards. Similar to applied morals, virtues are lived values, values in action, and they reflect one's human characteristics.
The famous Ancient Greek philosopher, Aristotle, defined moral virtue as the disposition to behave in the right manner and a mean (the golden mean) between two extremes of deficiency and excess, known as vices.

DEMYSTIFYING PURPOSE

Aristotle created a checklist (Aristotle's 12 Virtues) to understand the different virtues that one could cultivate or restrain in one's life.

The list of Aristotle's 12 virtues:

1. Bravery (courage)
2. Temperance (self-regulation)
3. Liberality (spending)
4. Magnificence (charisma)
5. Magnanimity (generosity)
6. Ambition (pride)
7. Patience (calmness)
8. Friendliness (humanity, compassion)
9. Truthfulness (honesty)
10. Wit (humour)
11. Modesty (ego)
12. Justice (doing the right thing)

'Virtue is the golden mean between two vices, the one of access and the other of deficiency.'

– Aristotle

DEMYSTIFYING PURPOSE

Virtues are about finding a balance (mean) between the vices of deficiency and excess. On either side of any virtue is a specific label when it is either excessive or deficient.

For example, too much bravery is rashness and too little is cowardice, too much temperance is ascetic and too little is addictive, too much truthfulness is boastfulness and too little is self-depreciation and so on.

To live virtuously is a process and it is not always easy, but generally speaking, virtues are the centrepieces that guide one to live a great and purposeful life.

Given below is my manifesto, which is an insight into my inner world and hopefully resonates with you:

> *"Follow your heart (values), acknowledge the ego (head) and let it go. Listen to your soul (intuition) and live morally well (virtues), making a difference and adding value as you grow"*
>
> *-Simone Maria Quinn*

DEMYSTIFYING PURPOSE

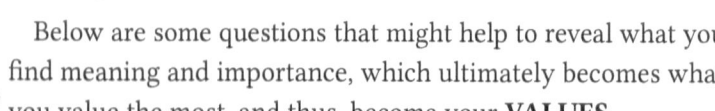

Below are some questions that might help to reveal what you find meaning and importance, which ultimately becomes what you value the most, and thus, become your **VALUES.**

Questions:

- What matters to you?
- What inspires you?
- What are you passionate about?
- What excites you?
- Who inspires you and why?
- What do you like spending your time doing?
- What do you like learning?
- When are you the happiest?
- Who do you love to be around?
- Where do you like to be?

'You decide what your values are in life and what you are going to do, and then you feel like you count, and that makes life worth living. It makes your life meaningful.'

- Annie Lennox

Part Three

Groundwork

Chapter 7: The Driver's Seat

'You want to be in the driver's seat of your own life because if you are not, life will drive you.'

- Oprah Winfrey

DEMYSTIFYING PURPOSE

Imagine your life as a car and the only way to make it move forward or backward or simply not move at all is in your hands - the driver in the driver's seat. Granted both the car and the driver may need a little assistance now and then over time, but as far as the direction and destination of one's journey is concerned, the car needs to be purposely driven by the driver.

This may sound pretty straightforward and completely doable, however it is often not the case, as the driver can be thrown off course, become lost, and feel dis-empowered, because nothing would be working due to the struggle of getting back on track.

Life is not easy at the best of times and one can easily be dislodged by unexpected events, experiences, distractions, influences, loss, pain, unresourceful actions, toxic environments, etc. Being or getting back on track of living a purposeful life on one's terms mainly depends on one's perspective, values, self-belief, and self-realization, and knowing that life matters and how one chooses to live it matters.

As an adult, being in the driver's seat is not just about setting goals and achieving them, but may also include setting personal targets to reach, ticking off the bucket list, or making dreams come true. It is also about the journey being relevant to the result or destination and considering why one does what they do, for what purpose, how they do it, and who for.

Up until recently, if I'd asked myself whether I have been in the driver's seat of my life, my answer would have been 'no'! I said 'no' because my path to my purpose was broken for a long time, when I let life happen to me as opposed to living life on my terms.

To be honest, I had been in a reactionary mode rather than being proactive regarding my decisions and choices because of my limiting self-beliefs, lack of self-love and compassion, and no connection with self.

For me, getting into the driver's seat of my life as an adult has involved a parallel journey of self-discovery, which was been hard and not always pretty. It seemed easy enough for me to say to myself that I will replace my limiting beliefs with self-empowering beliefs but it not that easy. It has taken a lot of self-work to believe and trust in myself and not fall back into the habits that had been serving me nothing.

When I finally consciously realized that we get one go at this life, my perception of life changed and I started asking myself better questions like: Why and what was I here to do? What did I want to achieve? What legacy did I want to leave? What needed to change?

'If you do anything too long that you're not in line with, eventually you're going hit a brick wall.'

- Simone Maria Quinn

In the next part of this chapter, I want to explore with you the three key areas that I found helpful in staying the course to pursuing a meaningful and purposeful life.

Those 3 key areas are:

1. Courage

2. Cause and Effect

DEMYSTIFYING PURPOSE

3. Self-Responsibility and Self-Accountability

1. Courage

'Courage does not roar. Sometimes courage is the quiet voice at the end of the day saying 'I will try again tomorrow.'

- Mary Anne Radmacher

Courage is the strength or the ability to make decisions, to take action, and keep on going when one feels a sense of uncertainty, having to facing an ordeal, or experiencing pain and or grief. With courage, one permits one's self to face difficulties despite the fear and the trepidation, and takes action anyway. Courage and fear go hand in hand in finding one's way through whatever that may be.

It has taken a great deal of courage for me to be self-accepting, self-trusting, and feel worthy given the emotional baggage, the diversions, the detours, and the choices that have been presented throughout my life, for example the beliefs, comparisons, expectations, wanting to belong, and being enough.

It has taken courage for me to be brave enough to stand in my own power and believe that I can do and achieve despite other people's ideas, stories, opinions, judgements, approval, or beliefs.

It has taken courage to be vulnerable, do the inner work, keep going, and connect with myself. It has taken courage to walk my path and to let go of what has held me back and has not or does not serve me well.

DEMYSTIFYING PURPOSE

I will always take strength from remembering that no one on the entire planet can do 'me' better than me and that I am stronger than I think.

'The courage to be is the courage to accept oneself, in spite of being unacceptable.'

-Paul Tillich

2. Cause and Effect

Cause and effect refer to the relationship between two events where one is the reason behind the other. The cause is the 'why' that makes the other event happen and the effect is the result (the 'what').

One can be living their life either 'at cause' or 'at effect', where 'at cause' one chooses to be self-empowered and 'at effect' one chooses to be self dis-empowered. Cause and effect are also known as living above or below the line of one's perspective on life, their responses, their decisions, and their actions.

If one was living their life at cause (or above the line), they would be making decisions based on positive self-beliefs and would be proactive, taking responsibility for outcomes. Being at cause is being in the driver's seat of life, where one would be living life rather than life happening to them.

If one was living their life at effect (or below the line), they would be making decisions based on limiting self-beliefs and would take a reactionary approach and not take responsibility for outcomes. Being at effect is not being the drivers of life and where life would be happening to one rather than one living life for themselves.

At cause response:

There was a time in my life where I'd been single for a long time, I was living alone and all I did was work and not much else. So, I decided that I need to take some action, take responsibility for where I was, and shift my perspective with regards to myself.

I knew that if anything was going to change so far as improving the quality of my life, where I could experience more joy and less angst, I was going to have to put myself in the driver's seat and make it happen.

I started to think more about what I wanted and how I wanted my life to be. The change began with me believing I was worthy and to start asking myself quality questions and to create more choices and make better decisions, which I did.

At effect response:

Let's take the same example of the time in my life where I'd been single for a long time, I was living alone and all I did was work and not much else. Instead of taking responsibility for where my life was at, I would look for excuses and blame others that my life was crap and that I had no choices.

I was waiting for good things to happen and for good luck would come my way. I would continue believing that I had nothing to look forward to and that was the way it was going to be for the rest of my life, i.e. not be in the driver's seat.

Stuff does just happen in life but depends on how one responds (rather than reacts) that is key to the outcomes or the results, the experiences, the quality of one's life, and ultimately, how one feels.

'Life is a perpetual instruction in cause and effect.'

- Ralph Waldo Emerson

3. Self-Responsibility and Self-Accountability

As one becomes an adult there is so much to take in and take on whilst navigating and living one's life day in day out. The earlier one can take the driver's role in their life, the better they'd be placed to navigate through all things in life and bounce back a lot more quickly when times aren't so good.

Self-responsibility and self-accountability are ultimate key tools needed in the pursuit of a purposeful life that is being driven by one who is sitting in the driver's seat.

Self-responsibility is one's ability to respond, take action, and having the capacity to consistently show up in life.

Self-accountability is one's ability to account for one's actions and to be answerable to oneself with regards to all matters in their life.

As I strive to succeed and be happy in every area of my life, I will inevitability make mistakes, I might fail and I may have to face being rejected as a part of the journey.

However, I know that the rewards make it all worthwhile and that I have the capacity and internal strength to handle all that I'll face.

DEMYSTIFYING PURPOSE

I believe one can embody self-responsibility and self-accountability by learning the lessons and working to improve themselves and by making a difference for the better, not only for self, but also for others.

'Your failures make your successes so much more meaningful'

- Guy Raz

Consider six ways to count on and be responsible for one's self:

1. Show up in the here and now and be present.

2. Stand in truth and be honest.

3. Stand solid and be disciplined with words and actions.

4. Be congruent and authentic in all areas of life.

5. Be open to not knowing everything and let go of the ego.

6. Be committed in action to grow.

'You are responsible for the world that you live in. It is not the government's responsibility. It is not your schools or your social club's or your church's or your neighbour's or your fellow citizen's. It is yours, utterly singularly yours.'

- August Wilson

Standing in one's power means being responsible and accounting for oneself whilst resourcefully doing the best one

DEMYSTIFYING PURPOSE

can on their life's journey despite the obstacles, distractions, loss, and misfortunes experienced.

It can take a lifetime to finally feel self-empowered, to sit in the driver's seat of one's life, driving forward with purpose, and most importantly, having fun while enjoying the ride along the way.

DEMYSTIFYING PURPOSE

Some journal prompts to consider:

- How has your journey been so far?

- What does being in the driver's seat look like for you?

- What story are you telling yourself and how is it serving you?

- Would you like to change the story?

- Who do you need to be?

- What does life look like going forward?

'You're in charge of it, you were born with it, so take the ball and run with it!'

- Simone Maria Quinn

Chapter 8: Awakening Potential

'What the caterpillar calls the end of the world, the master calls a butterfly.'

- Richard Bach

DEMYSTIFYING PURPOSE

When it comes to people, potential may be referred to as an ability currently not realized and where one can be or become or achieve something in the future.

I believe that purpose and potential go hand in hand, where the purpose is realized is where potential can exist. The purpose is the pursuit of something meaningful and potential is realizing what is possible or what one is capable of achieving or becoming. The rewards could be endless where one's potential is realized, such as personal growth and development and an increase in self-awareness, self-belief, self-motivation, self-fulfilment and happiness, and a connection with self-identity.

Awakening or discovering potential doesn't just happen overnight for most people. It may take time to recognise, acknowledge and unleash, and like with purpose, everyone's potential is unique and can flourish if given the right environment, opportunities, resources, encouragement, and support.

Some people may never discover or awaken their potential in their lifetime for a multitude of reasons, as the 'getting through life' gets in the way. It is not uncommon to hear the phrase 'She/He never reached her/his full potential' or 'If only they'd realized their potential' concerning others' observations and opinions.

If one knows whether they have the ability or not to do something, why is it that they may lack the interest, inspiration, motivation, or fortitude to pursue what could be possible? Having already mentioned the environment, opportunity, encouragement, and support, one's internal world plays a big role too. Fear of not being good enough, fear of failing and not fulfilling other's expectations, self-doubt, and lack of self-belief can wreak havoc if left untamed.

'Our deepest fear is not that we are inadequate.
Our deepest fear is that we are powerful beyond our measure.'
– Marianne Williamson

Imagine what one's life might look like if their potential is awakened, unleashed, and pursued, thus presenting all sorts of possibilities, opportunities, and experiences beyond imagination.

> **Purpose + Potential = Meaningful Life = Story of One's Life**

I've kept the door closed with regard to realizing my potential over the years, because I have not been connected with my purpose.
It is almost like I've been in a daze chasing my tail and living at effect where I was constantly reacting to circumstances and hoping to be saved.

For so long, I carried the limiting beliefs that I was not good enough and that I did not belong, which weighed so heavily, and every time an opportunity came up I'd look for a reason or an excuse as to why I wouldn't do it and I'd even procrastinate with making any decision. I've come to realize that self-belief is the key to achieving anything because, no matter how many failures, distractions, and challenges, or other's opinions are encountered, self-belief is what drives one forward through change and growth.

DEMYSTIFYING PURPOSE

As I am connecting with my purpose these days and interpret my life differently, I have opened the door to my potential and I now dare to dream and create a vision for myself knowing that I am worthy. Having come from a place of emptiness and despair, I now know how empowering living with purpose and realizing potential can be, and that, a meaningful life is what mine will be.

'Just like purpose, an infinite potential is already hidden within you. It's only a matter of awakening it.'

– Simone Maria Quinn

The question is how does one know their potential and how do they awaken or unleash it?
Everyone is born with gifts and talents and it is a matter of tapping into them and using them for one's self and contributing and adding value to others.

In the next part of this chapter, l will explore the Be-Do-Have model with regards to being a useful tool on the journey of discovering one's potential whilst on the quest for purposeful living. The Be-Do-Have model has been around for a very long time and I have only recently begun to appreciate its simplicity and effectiveness.

Be-Do-Have simply means one has to be in order to do before one can have.

BE:

'If you plan on being anything less than you are capable of being, you will probably be unhappy all the days of your life.'

- Abraham Maslow

DEMYSTIFYING PURPOSE

Start from a place of being! The 'be' part is about whether one is truly being themselves and are they being and who they need to be to step into their authentic self. When one is being their authentic self, they are aligned with being what they feel, think, want, and how they act.

To be is to embody everything that is the manifestation of what one desires to be and achieve, therefore, the best possible authentic version of themselves.

One must first start from a state of being before one starts the doing. It takes courage to stand and be all that one is and own the true stories of who they are, given the never-ending challenges, distractions, pain, and fear that one faces in life.

If one denies who one truly is, the pain and the fear will start to take ownership and so will the stories that one would be telling themselves.

By working on a state of being interested and being aware of self and connecting and believing with self, one can begin to tap into their gifts and talents and move towards unleashing one's potential.

Along with one's thoughts and intellect, daring to dream and using one's imagination are also key tools for tapping into one's creativity and to open up the gateway of what is possible with regards to encompassing, embracing, and expressing all that one is and aspires to be.

Some questions to ask oneself around Being:

- Who am I?

DEMYSTIFYING PURPOSE

- Who do I want to be?
- What is important?
- What matters?
- What do I value?
- What can I improve on?
- What is meaningful?
- What am I thankful for?
- How can I be in order to do?

DO:

'Find out who you are and do it on purpose.'

- Dolly Parton

When one is being they can see more clearly what it is they need to do regarding their passion and start to take purposeful action to realize it. Doing is the intentional living part of being, where one will create the possibility to have what they manifested and realizing their potential with ease of flow moving forward through life.

With an open mind and a sense of curiosity, one can think about how to do the doing and start asking themselves questions with regards to the same because it is in the doing where one finds out and witnesses the changes within.

There is no perfect way in the doing, as mistakes will be made and there will be failures for various reasons. But, as long as one keeps on learning and moving forward from a place of being, one will experience joy, happiness, and satisfaction consistently on their journey of doing.

Coming from an embodied and empowered state of being, below are some questions around 'Doing':

- What is the first step?

- What are my goals and aspirations?

- What are the action steps?

- What do I need to do?

- What do I need help with?

- Who could I ask?

- What do I need to work on?

- What do I need to let go of?

- What else?

HAVE:

'Until you make peace with who you are, you'll never be content with what you have.'

- Doris Mortman

There is some logic in thinking that if one is living life from a place of having, then they will be happy and that they will travel through life with ease. However, as already discussed, if one is living life from a place of being, then one will have a more fulfilling and meaningful life, living authentically and on purpose.

Having is not just about reaching goals, attaining results, and acquiring stuff. Having is also about whether one is living aligned with their values, feeling connected to self and others, and being at peace with what they have as what they had wished for.

Where one is being, doing, and having all that they manifested, it would be reasonable to assume they would be experiencing fun, love, joy, and fulfilment in their life.

For me, it goes without saying that if one is in such a place internally and coming from a place of meaning, then to give, to contribute, and to add value to others would be a natural progression that would be a win-win for the greater good of all that be.

DEMYSTIFYING PURPOSE

Some questions to ask oneself around 'Having':

- What do I want?
- What will I have?
- How will I know when I have it?
- How will I be feeling?
- What are the outcomes?
- What does my life look like?
- Will I have the life I want?
- How will I be serving, contributing, and giving to others?
- What legacy will I leave?

Journal prompt:

To give yourself some space to answer some of the questions from the '**Be - Do - Have**' sections above.

Make sure you are in a comfortable place where your mind is quiet and that your external environment is in silence too, without any interruptions.

DEMYSTIFYING PURPOSE

The following is an inspirational poem regarding the importance of believing in yourself and your dreams and becoming who you want to be.

You Can Be Whatever You Want To Be
(By poet: Donna Levine)

There is inside you
All of the potential
To be whatever you want to be;
All of the energy
To do whatever you want to do.
Imagine yourself as you would like to be,
Doing what you want to do,
And each day, take one step
Towards your dream.
And though at times it may seem too
Difficult to continue,
Hold on to your dream.
One morning you will awake to find
That you are the person you dreamed of,
Doing what you wanted to do,
Simply because you had the courage
To believe in your potential
And to hold on to your dream.

Part Four

Gifts

Chapter 9: Change - The Seed of Growth

'Change is hard at first, messy in the middle and gorgeous at the end.'

- Unknown

DEMYSTIFYING PURPOSE

The topic of change is immense which can be covered on various levels and is a subject worth devoting a whole book to. However, in this chapter, I will be focusing on change concerning one's purpose and how we can respond to change that influences our life experiences and personal growth.

Change is a variation in the way things are done or altered that makes something different from what one used to be. Change can be sudden and unexpected or it is proactively sorted after. Change can occur slowly or quickly as an immediate response to an occurrence or an event.

Given the different stages of life one experiences, change will not only occur on mental, emotional and spiritual level, but a physical level too, as one ages throughout their life. The interesting and fascinating part is how one responds and adapts to the challenges that change presents. Sometimes change can be pretty extreme and painful and the only way out of it is by living through it and getting to the other side.

What triggers change? Some examples of external factors that can trigger change are loss, grief, abuse, violence, separation, fractured families, homelessness, environment, pandemics, economic, financial, unemployment, social differences, disagreements, unrest, and war, etc.

Alongside external factors, various internal factors can trigger change too, such as one's thoughts, feelings, emotions, and beliefs, that can influence one's reaction or response to what is going on externally and internally.

This brings me to the purpose and the internal shift that

DEMYSTIFYING PURPOSE

is required if one seeks to change or where one has given themselves an ultimatum to change or else nothing will change. Things will stay the same when nothing changes, stagnation can start to set in; and thus; limit one's options regarding personal growth, joy, fulfilment, and pursuing a meaningful life.

With regards to connecting to purpose, one needs to be able to handle uncertainty and change in one's stride and keep learning from the good and the hard times. For some, the road is longer and more difficult than for others, given that each individual is on a different route with a unique set of circumstances to navigate and contend with.

'For one's life to change one needs to change. Nothing changes, until you change.
Everything changes, once you change.'

- Julian Lennon

I have experienced a lot of change through my life with regards to external factors, e.g. family circumstances, living locations, working environments, travel, separation, loss, grief, economical challenges, and, of course, ageing. Some of these changes I have been the architect of and some I have not. Over time, I have managed to adapt with regards to change, even when it seemed too painful to bear and when I was at my lowest. As a result, I have built up my resilience muscle that has kept me going and getting on with the mechanics of life, but internally, I've not always given myself the time or space to just be, and to feel and heal.

DEMYSTIFYING PURPOSE

I think it would be fair to say that I've been in combat internally with change most of my life simply because I had disconnected from myself and would just keep operating from this default position. On one hand, I could handle uncertainty, but on the other, I wanted certainty, stability, self-acceptance, and belonging.

In recent years, I have purposefully experienced a lot of transformational change, because I was ready too and that I knew I had to change my internal world and move forward in my life to keep growing and evolving one step at a time and find the equilibrium within.

The next part of this chapter explores four key areas that one might encounter when dealing with change when one is in pursuit of something meaningful, living purposefully, and in alignment with their values.

Those four key areas are:

1. Challenges, Opportunities, and Perspective

2. Resistance to Change

3. Embracing Change

4. Grow and Evolve

1. Challenges, Opportunities and Perspective

'Challenges are what make life interesting and overcoming them is what makes life meaningful.'

- Joshua J Marine

DEMYSTIFYING PURPOSE

Change can be a challenge within itself. In a pursuit to connecting to the purpose and living a value-driven meaningful life, one will experience a change in one form or another and will undoubtedly be met with challenges along the way. Some challenges or obstacles could set one back to a point where one must access and re-evaluate whether they are on the right track or not.

I have found that sometimes challenges or setbacks may open the door to other options and opportunities that weren't there before, which can take one on a completely different path towards their purpose. For me, it has been about learning how to take the setbacks in my stride, to build my self-trust muscle, to continue moving forward, however challenging, and to remember that, instead of trying to be perfect, I just keep trying.

If one has a purpose in their life they are more likely to have a healthier outlook on life and be able to shift their perspective with more ease and make better decisions when faced with challenges. I think that perspective is a very handy tool, because it allows one to look at something and make it mean what they want it to mean, thus affecting their perception of reality. Changing perspective is not always easy but it allows one to resourcefully focus on and work through the challenges, and, by doing so, open up one's paths for moving forward rather than standing still.

'Do the best you can until you know better. Then when you know better, do better.'

-Maya Angelou

2. Resistance to Change

'Change is never painful. Only resistance to change is painful.'

- Gautama Buddha

Change can bring with it a lot of uncertainty and discomfort, and so, resisting it is a common response particularly if one needs certainty in their life. One can fear change because they don't know what is on its other side (i.e. what will happen and will they be okay?). So, instead of experiencing the perceived pain, they'd rather stick with what they know and feel comfortable with.

To change, one is required to step out of or expand their comfort zone and face their fears while doing it. If one does not take a leap of faith now and again, they will never know what they are capable of and stay stuck, and will never be the best version of themselves.

On many occasions in my life, I have had to dig deep within myself to deal with my resistance and face my fears in stepping into being who I need to be, to change the status quo I was willing to accept at the time. Nowadays, I am aware and more equipped, so I don't need to dig too deeply when facing my resistance because I am more open to embracing what it is I fear.

'Resistance is the step to change.'

- Louise Hay

3. Embracing Change - Resilience

'Everything changes with time, but somewhere, situations also makes you to change.'

- Sisira Sivaraj

Change is constantly occurring and there are things in life we can't change, like ageing. If one embraces the fact that they are ageing every day of their life, then it stands to reason that they might see every day as a blessing and use it purposefully.

By embracing and going with the flow of the change process, one is better placed to adapt and learn from what they experience and build resilience. Resilience assists one to cope with the challenges and the waves of change that may emerge and helps one bounce back quickly from the difficulties experienced in life.

'When we learn to become resilient, we learn to embrace the beautifully broad spectrum of the human experience.'

- Jaeda Dewalt

4. Grow and Evolve

'We do not grow absolutely, chronologically. We grow sometimes in one dimension, and not in another; unevenly. We grow partially. We are relative. We are mature in one realm, childish in another. The past, present, and future mingle and pull us backward, forward, or fix us in the present. We are made up of layers, cells, constellations.'

- Anais Nin

DEMYSTIFYING PURPOSE

Change is the seed of growth because, just like the wind, change (intentional or unforeseen) can disrupt the landscape of life that one can either embrace or resist.

Where one desires purposeful change in their life for whatever reason, they can do that by setting targeted and specific goals to attain the change and outcome.

Targeted goals are important because they facilitate the change where one is engaging in the process of growth. Growth is a perpetual need of the human condition and when one is growing, they will evolve into who they want to be.

To evolve is to keep exploring, expanding one's horizons, learning, taking action, growing and embracing the change within and around oneself as one moves forward through the finite amount of time they have in life.

DEMYSTIFYING PURPOSE

12 Tips for coping with change and growth:

1. Acknowledge the change.
2. Face your fears, thoughts, and feelings.
3. Look after your health (mind, body, and soul).
4. Show yourself kindness and compassion.
5. Reach out and communicate; talk to someone you feel comfortable with.
6. Keep an open mind.
7. Embrace the change and adapt.
8. Look for the opportunities.
9. Take action; one step at a time (i.e. responses, decisions, goals),
10. Keep learning.
11. Be present.
12. Be the change.

'Growth is uncomfortable because you've never been there before. You've never seen this version of you.
So give yourself a little grace and breathe through it.'

-Kristi

Chapter 10: A Meaningful Life

'Life is never made unbearable by circumstances, but only by lack of meaning and purpose.'

- Viktor Frankl

DEMYSTIFYING PURPOSE

A meaningful life is a life lived with purpose - purpose being the why that drives one forward when they are connected to themselves as well as being fulfilled and satisfied because meaning is present. To have meaning is to feel a sense of belonging and significance, to find something good that sustains one, and to serve beyond one's self with interest and keen awareness.

The purpose of life is to pursue something meaningful to achieve a state of happiness. Happiness, in itself, is not fulfilment - it comes and goes. Where there is a lack of meaning, purpose, and fulfilment, one may experience a lack of happiness and joy. One could also experience a lack of engagement, lack of motivation, dissatisfaction, despair, sadness, anxiety, and emptiness.

'A meaningful life is fulfilling and brings happiness. Happiness is not fulfilling and does not bring with it meaning, it is a state of being that comes and goes.'

- Simone Maria Quinn

It takes inspiration, dedication, and personal work to live a meaningful life. I believe that it is an ongoing process as one grows and evolves creating and living one's life. Meaningfulness is the guiding light that shines hope that gives one something to hold on to when life is really good and when times are not so good.

What is meaningful will be different for everyone since we all interpret the same thing differently based on our mind maps. What one pursues as meaningful may not be understood by others, it may not please others and may not get the approval of others and vice versa. The thing is, if one pursues others' opinions or interpretations of what is meaningful, then one is putting their life on pause until the time comes when one chooses to press the play button and pursue what they find meaningful instead.

We all are here for different reasons that are unique and significant and it is for those reasons why we all belong and contribute and make a difference in a way no one else can.
It takes courage and may require some sacrifices to pursue what is meaningful, but, at the end of the day, the only person one needs to convince, please, and be happy with is oneself and everything will fall into place as it will, including the quality of the relationships with the people that surround one. Pursuing what is meaningful and living with purpose are the antidotes to feeling unworthy, dis-empowered, and empty.

When I look back on life there have been some times where I felt I had meaning or there was meaning in my life, but overall, I wouldn't say that I had been consciously pursuing something meaningful, living purposefully, and feeling fulfilled.

I have been on a long and uneasy journey from restlessness to connecting with my purpose and to now living a meaningful life where I am pursuing things of meaning to me.
I am at a point in my life where I have come to terms with the fact that I have taken many detours, that I have embraced my uniqueness, that I am enough, my 'why' is everything, I can identify with myself, I listen to intuition, I am in the driver's seat, I acknowledge my potential, I want to keep growing and evolving and to live a meaningful life and to contribute and make

DEMYSTIFYING PURPOSE

a difference on my journey ahead of me.

'Once you learn what life is about, there is no way to erase the knowledge.
If you try something else with your life, you will always sense that you are missing something.'

– James Redfield

The next part of this chapter explores 3 elements with regards to fostering and sustaining a meaningful life when one is connected or has reconnected to one's purpose and where living one's passions become a reality.

The 3 elements are:

1. Live your truth

2. Purpose

3. Sharing your wisdom and storytelling

1. Live Your Truth:

'The best way to know yourself is to have the courage to observe yourself, accept yourself, and realize that you're right in front of yourself.'

- Jim Fortin

To embody a meaningful life one needs to live one's truth by living their values, acting with integrity and congruency, and having compassion for self and others.

With regards to myself, it has taken a lot of courage and bravery to get to know, accept and embrace myself to connect with my purpose and create a life to live on my terms and face all my fears whilst navigating life itself.

Leading from a place of love and quietening, the voice of the ego has helped me to let go of what did not serve and of what has already happened that can't be changed.

Leading from the heart has made it easier for me to connect and bond with others and establish healthier relationships. All these connections have helped with my sense of belonging where I feel valued for who I am and that I am enough.

'You can't live a meaningful life without truth as your guide.'

-Carlos Del Valle

2. Purpose:

'The key to purpose is finding your strength to serve others...Embracing the painful memories can lead to new insights and wisdom to finding the good that sustains you.'

- Emily Esfahani Smith

The purpose is all about what drives one forward and gives one vitality. It is about pursuing what one is passionate about, interested in, and is of value not only to self but also others. It is also about finding out what one is good at - one's potential - and using it to serve others and make a difference.

Purpose allows one to use their imagination, make better decisions and choices, re-evaluate, face challenges and adapt, be open to new possibilities, and create new projects with a sense of freedom. When connected with their purpose one steps into one's self who is focused and is clear about what matters, what is meaningful, and life just makes sense.

I know that I am on purpose when I am pursuing and doing what is meaningful to me. Whether this task be paid work, unpaid work, voluntary work, acts of love, hobbies or simply being creative, I can go about setting small goals to realize my dreams and to keep learning and improving myself, bringing happiness into my life and the lives of others.

'The good life consists in deriving happiness by using your signature strengths every day in the main realms of living. The meaningful life adds one more component: using these same strengths to forward knowledge, power or goodness.'

- Martin Seligman

3. Sharing Your Wisdom and Story Telling:

'Life is sentimental. Why should I be cold and hard about it? That's the main content.
The biggest thing in people's lives is their loves and dreams and visions, you know.'

- Jim Harrison

Connecting with others either directly or indirectly is an integral aspect of living a meaningful life. What one pursues, achieves, and contributes throughout their life will cause ripple effects, which will impact and influence others in one way or another.

DEMYSTIFYING PURPOSE

One's life is made is up of chapters capturing the story of their life they have already lived. The chapters that are still to be written will become the stories that one chooses to tell - dictated by the decisions, choices, and actions taken in one's life.
The idea that one can create a vision of how they'd like their life to be and to take the actions to achieve it is quite a powerful one.

'What you think you become. What you imagine you create.'

- Buddha

The depth and detail of the story of one's life will determine the impact and significance of the difference that one will have made in one life, thus shaping the legacy one leaves. The stories will include a whole gamete of experiences, including successes, failures, loss, grief, ups, and downs. Hopefully, there would be some lessons, learnings, and wisdom gathered along the way to be acknowledged and shared for the benefit of one and of others. Are you the author of your life, and if so, what does the next chapter of your life look like and feel like and how will it read?

'You must have control of the authorship of your own destiny. The pen that writes your life story must be held in your own hand.'

- Irene C Kassorla

About what has been covered in this book, pursuing something meaningful is about joining all the dots, doing the internal work, and taking action so that, as one connects to their purpose, they live a life that is meaningful to them.

DEMYSTIFYING PURPOSE

Some useful tips I have acquired for sustaining a meaningful life:

- Believing in yourself starts with you.

- Improve yourself by setting goals for yourself...one step at a time.

- Be curious.

- Be hungry for information and keep learning.

- Engage in life.

- Check-in with yourself and get some quiet time with yourself.

- Develop a vision for yourself.

- Pursue things of value, what you are good at and which is useful.

- Don't let excuses get in the way. Find a way, do it, and move forward.

- Make a difference and remember that life is not just about self, it is also about others.

- Freedom will be obtained from being disciplined.

- Come from a place of gratitude.

- Look for joy and be fulfilled.

- Live to your full potential.

- Who is writing your story and what will be your legacy?

My Favourite Quotes

'So-called 'late-bloomers' get a bad rap. Sometimes the people with the greatest potential often take the longest to find their path because their sensitivity is a double-edged sword- it lives at the heart of their brilliance, but it also makes them more susceptible to life's pains. Good thing we aren't being penalized for handing in our purpose late. The soul doesn't know a thing about deadlines.'

-Jeff Brown (from 'Love It Forward')

'Because of routines that we follow, we often forget that life is an ongoing adventure...and the sooner we realize that the quicker we will be able to treat life as art: to bring all our energies to each encounter, to remain flexible enough to notice that and admit when what we expected to happen did not happen. We need to remember that we are created creative and can invent new scenarios as frequently as they are needed.'

- Maya Angelou

DEMYSTIFYING PURPOSE

'We all have a purpose,
A mission, that, we have been
Pursuing without being fully aware of it,
and once we bring it completely into consciousness,
our lives can take off.'

– *James Redfield (from 'Celestine Prophecy')*

'If you want to be a true professional,
you will do something outside yourself.
Something to repair tears in your community
Something to make life a little better for people less fortunate than you.
That's what I think a meaningful life is - living not for oneself, but for one's community.'

- *Ruth Bader Ginsburg*

REFERENCES:

'Five Pathways to Purpose' (23/01/2020) by Martha Beck (Article)

'Enoughness' by Alison Robertson (Article)

'Do You Know Your 'Why' – 4 Questions to Find Your Purpose' Blog by Margie Warrell (30/10/2013)

'Why Having a Strong 'Why' Statement is the Key to Staying Motivated and Focused' (08/03/2017) by Nancy A Ruffin (Article)

'10 Things That Make A Person Unique' Blog by Jack Nollan (A Conscious Rethink)

'Ego vs Intuition: Learning how to identify your inner voices' by Resilient Educator (The Share Team)

'Relationship between Values and Virtues' (25/01/2018) by Jack Krupansky (Article)

'Self-responsibility/Self-accountability Qualifies You as An Adult' by Will Joel Friedman (Ph.D.) (Blog)

'What makes a people pleaser?' Blog by Anne Stoneson from Labyrinth Healing

'10 Life Purpose Tips To Help You Find Your Purpose' Blog by Jack Canfield

About the Author

Simone is a human behaviour enthusiast who is keenly interested in personal empowerment. Simone has worked as a coach in the areas of life skills, change and personal development. Her personal mission is to assist people who want to connect with their purpose so they can use their newfound awareness to live a fulfilled and meaningful life. Simone is also an experienced and creative Chef with 30 years of experience and 'Demystifying Purpose' is Simone's bold attempt at translating her rich culinary experience into practical life wisdom!

www.ingramcontent.com/pod-product-compliance
Lightning Source LLC
Chambersburg PA
CBHW020326010526
44107CB00054B/1996